The LIFE CYCLE of a PRAYING MANTIS

Andrew Hipp
Photography by Dwight Kuhn

The Rosen Publishing Group's
PowerKids Press™
New York

For Sue Bluebird and all of her animal stories—Andrew Hipp
To Matthew—Dwight Kuhn

Published in 2002 by The Rosen Publishing Group, Inc.
29 East 21st Street, New York, NY 10010

First Edition

Book Design: Michael Caroleo and Michael de Guzman
Project Editor: Emily Raabe

The author gratefully acknowledges Kerry Katovich, who reviewed an early draft of this book.

Photo Credits: All photos © Dwight Kuhn.

Hipp, Andrew.
The life cycle of a praying mantis / Andrew Hipp.
       p. cm. — (The life cycles library)
Includes bibliographical references and index.
ISBN 0-8239-5867-1 (lib. bdg.)
1. Praying mantis—Juvenile literature. [1. Praying mantis.] I. Title.
QL508.M2 H56 2002
595.7'27—dc21
                                                                    2001000149

Manufactured in the United States of America

Contents

Hatching in Spring

In late spring, 50 to 400 praying mantises hatch from a single egg case. Each baby mantis is in a clear, thin sac that hangs from the egg case. The babies fight their way out of the sacs. Each one climbs a thread to the top of the egg case or onto a nearby branch. The praying mantises, also called mantids, wait for a few hours as their soft, **transparent** skin darkens and hardens into a shell. The mantids may be eaten by lizards, spiders, frogs, ants, or even other mantids!

◀ *These baby mantids have just hatched. They still have the soft, transparent skin they had at birth.*

5

Young Nymphs

Praying mantises are called nymphs from the time they leave the egg case until they are full-grown adults. Like adults, mantid nymphs are good hunters. They also hide from animals that might eat them. When they are in danger, mantid nymphs press themselves to the ground. Their brown or green bodies help to hide them. After hiding like this for a moment, nymphs may scurry away to safety. They cannot fly yet because their wings are not fully grown.

Mantid nymphs spend their time eating insects and staying away from animals that might eat them. They can eat as many as three crickets in a day. ▶

Changes While Growing

Insects, like all other **arthropods**, have an **exoskeleton**. An exoskeleton is a hard shell that covers an insect's body. It acts like a suit of armor. Like armor, an exoskeleton cannot change in size. Insects must shed their exoskeletons as they grow, a process called **molting**. After molting, an insect must wait for a new exoskeleton to harden. Molting is a part of **metamorphosis**. During metamorphosis, mantids change from egg to nymph, then from nymph to adult.

◄ *This mantid has just completed a molt. Mantid nymphs go through four or more molts before they are adults.*

Just Before Adulthood

After four molts, a praying mantis nymph is almost ready to become an adult. In size and shape, the nymph looks like an adult. It is still a nymph, however. At this size, nymphs sometimes face their **predators**, rear up, and open their jaws. They may raise their front legs and make a threatening sound. Large mantid nymphs may even **lunge** at their predators. Mantid nymphs sometimes scare off predators much larger than themselves.

Instead of full-grown wings, this mantid nymph has wing pads. These are tiny wings that are too small for flying. ▶

Final Molt

In late summer or early fall, after four or five molts, a praying mantis undergoes its last molt and becomes an adult praying mantis. The final molt from nymph to adult takes 3 to 5 minutes. The mantid's exoskeleton cracks open, allowing the mantid to pull free its body, legs, and **antennae**. The mantid must have plenty of room for the molt to be successful. If it does not have enough room in which to stretch its old exoskeleton, the mantid may die.

The mantid's exoskeleton splits open, allowing the mantid to come out. The adult mantid clings to a branch and unfolds its wings.

Adulthood

ale adult mantids don't eat much because they do not need to produce eggs and egg sacs. Instead, they spend their time wandering about, looking for mates. All of their movement makes the males more visible to predators such as birds and bats. The female mantids eat while the males look for mates. In the first two weeks of adulthood, female mantids may double their body weight. Females use much of the food they eat to make eggs.

Adult female mantids can be from 2 to 4 inches (5 to 10 cm) long. ▶

Waiting and Preying

A mantid rarely **stalks** its prey. Instead, it remains perfectly still, waiting for prey to pass by. The praying mantis is almost invisible in the brush or grass. When an insect passes by, the mantid's forelegs dart out suddenly and grab it. Then the mantid bites through the back of the neck to kill its prey. Mantids will go searching for prey only if they have not eaten in a very long time. Like most insects, adult mantids can survive for days without food.

◄ *Mantids usually eat small insects, like this grasshopper. Sometimes, though, they attack mice, salamanders, or even hummingbirds!*

Mating

A female praying mantis can mate about two weeks after she becomes an adult. She may produce a smelly substance, called a **pheromone**. A male that smells the pheromone flies to her. He is careful, as female mantids often attack and eat males. The male sneaks closer, then jumps onto the female's back. They mate for 2 hours or longer. Sometimes the female chews off the male's head while they mate! Mantids can live for days without their heads.

This male (at far right) needs to be careful so that the larger female does not bite off his head! ▶

Laying Eggs

When she is ready to lay eggs, the female builds a nest called an egg case. She builds it from a gluelike **protein** made inside her own body. The female uses the tip of her **abdomen** to whip air into the protein. This whipped air creates pockets in the egg case. The female puts her eggs in these air pockets. The egg case is hard when it dries. The female mantis may have time to build six or more egg cases in one season. When winter comes, she will die.

◀ *This egg case will protect the eggs until spring. Then the eggs inside will hatch, and hundreds of nymphs will come out.*

Looking for Mantids

While a mantid waits for prey, it holds its front legs together as though in prayer. This is why mantids often are called praying mantises. In spring, when egg cases begin to open, you may find praying mantises on window screens. Look for them in the kinds of places where you find grasshoppers, such as in fields or along roadsides. Keep your eyes open for egg cases at all times of the year. If you find one, come back often to watch it. One day in spring or early summer, you may see hundreds of praying mantis nymphs coming out of their egg sacs.

Glossary

abdomen (AB-duh-min) The large, rear section of an insect's body.

antennae (an-TEH-nee) Rodlike organs on insects' heads used to smell and feel.

arthropods (AR-thruh-podz) Animals that have an exoskeleton instead of bones inside their bodies.

exoskeleton (ek-soh-SKEH-leh-tin) The hard outer shell of an arthropod's body.

lunge (LUNJ) To rush forward.

metamorphosis (meh-tuh-MOR-fuh-sis) The series of changes that an insect undergoes when it molts.

molting (MOHLT-ing) Shedding skin, feathers, or exoskeleton.

pheromone (FEHR-uh-mohn) A substance, much like a perfume, made by an insect or other animal.

predators (PREH-duh-terz) Animals that kill other animals for food.

protein (PROH-teen) One of the most important substances found in living things.

stalks (STAWKS) Follows something closely and secretly.

transparent (tranz-PEHR-ent) Able to be seen through, like a window.

Index

Web Sites

To learn more about praying mantises, check out these Web sites:

www.jps.net/meel/mantis/

www.insecta-inspecta.com/mantids/praying/